At the Fair

Written by Jade Michaels

Illustrated by Daron Parton

Bronto and Beaver went to the fair.

3

They went up on a horse.
They like going up
on a horse.

5

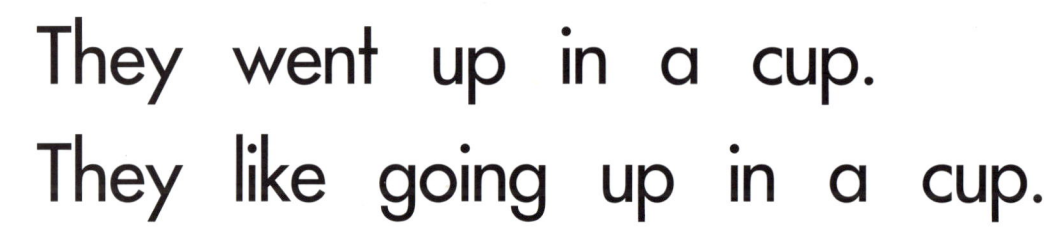

They went up in a cup.
They like going up in a cup.

7

They went up in a jet.
They like going up in a jet.

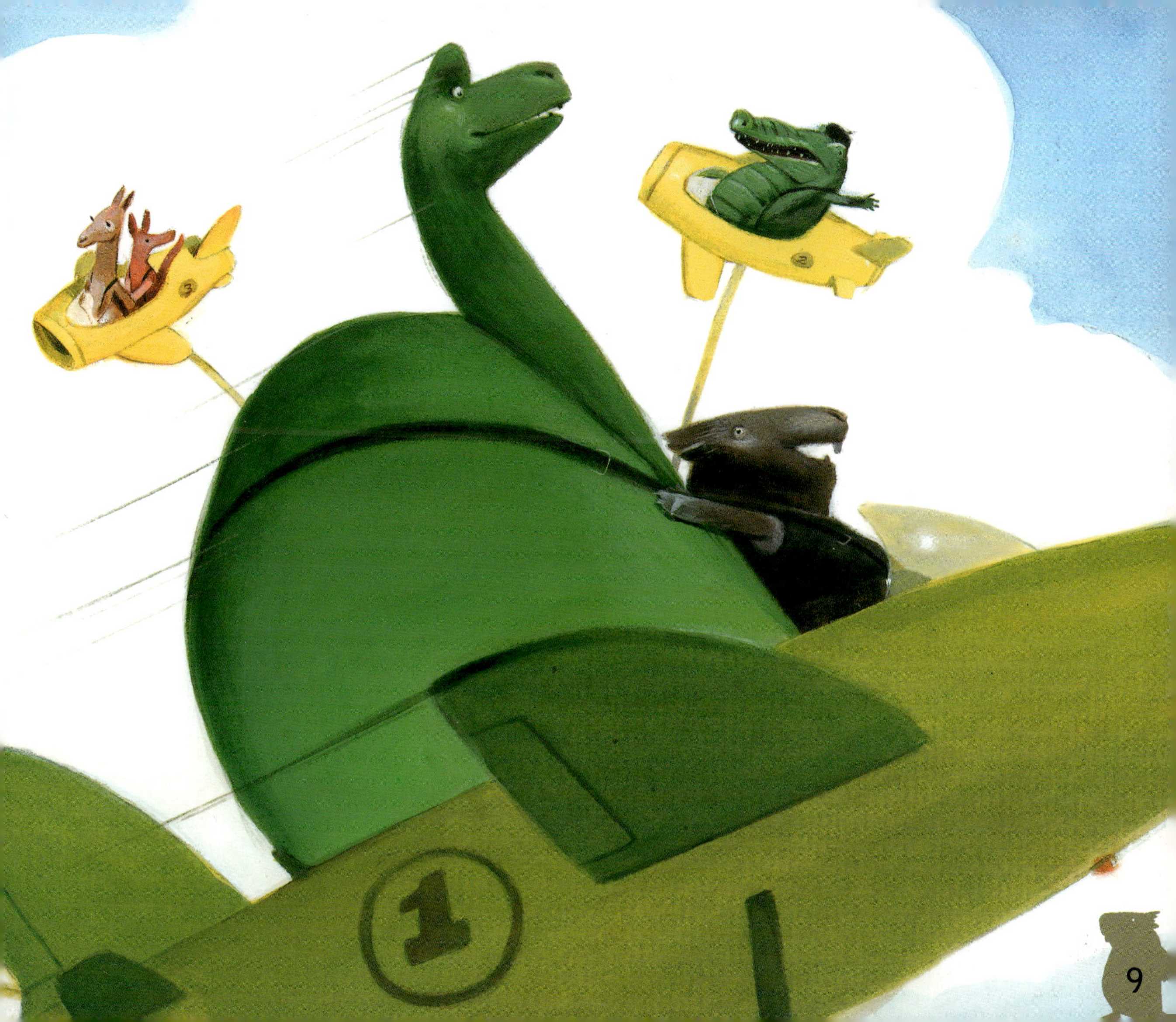

They went up on a train.

11

The train went up
and up and up.

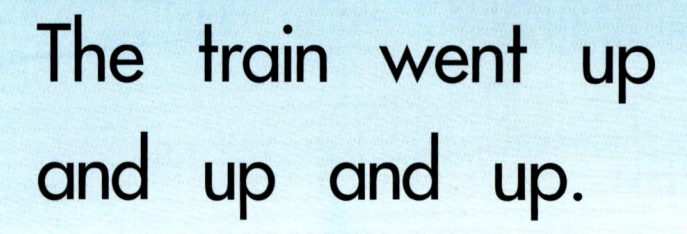

13

The train went down and down and down.

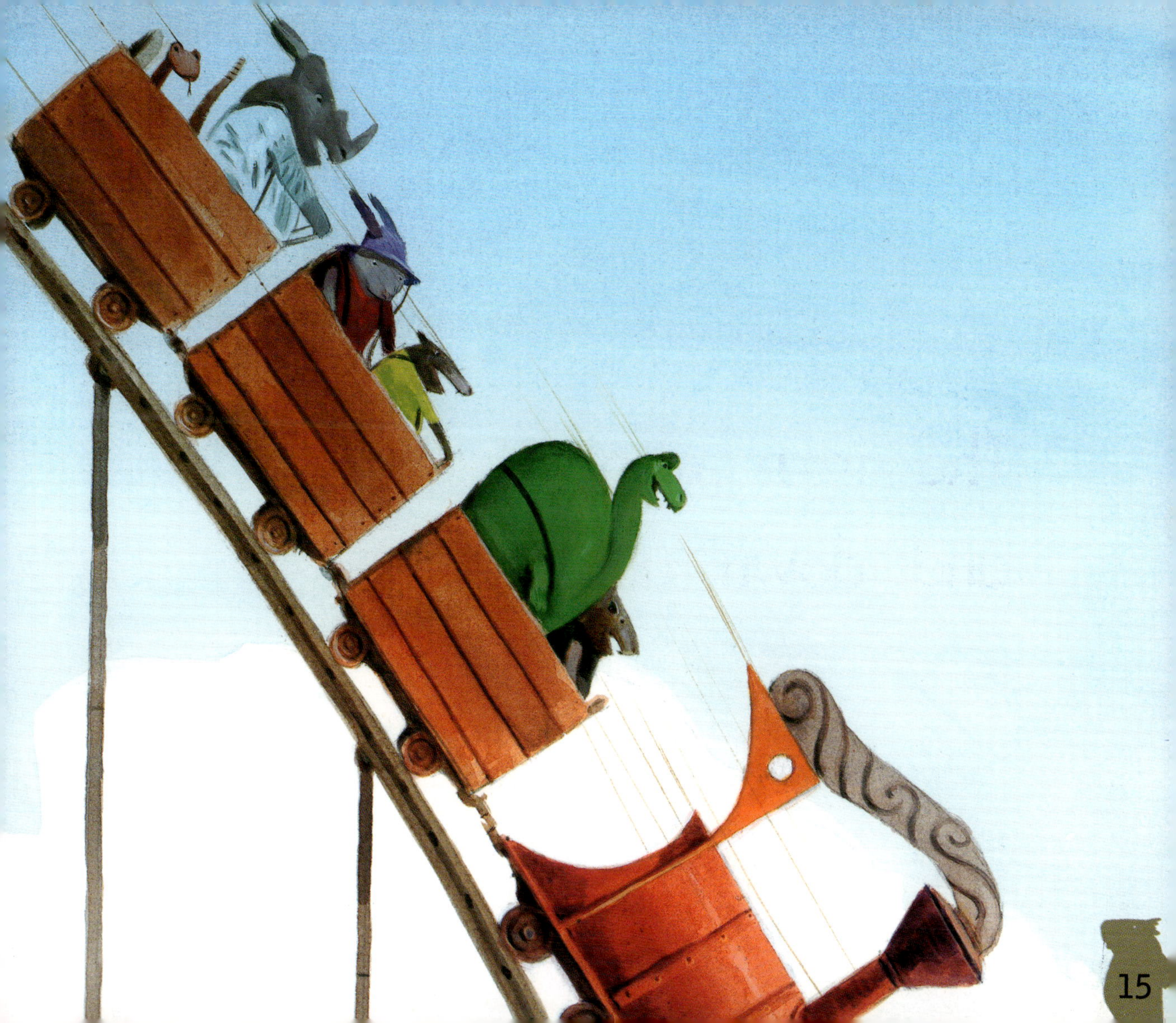

"We like this train," said Beaver and Bronto.